You're Invited

A WEEK OF FAMILY DEVOTIONS ON THE LORD'S SUPPER

You're Invited

FAITH
ALIVE®
Christian Resources

**John Bouwers, Karen De Boer, S. R. Larin,
and Leonard Vander Zee**

introduction

This five-day devotional was written for families to learn and wonder about the Lord's Supper together. Designed to be used with children who are in different places along their faith journey—those considering participation in the Lord's Supper, those who have already been participating in it, those who are ready to learn more—it's a devotional you can return to again and again. For example, you may find it helpful to use all or some of these devotions as a way to prepare for the Lord's Supper together before a communion service or around the celebration of Easter.

The first devotional talks about our invitation—our invitation from Jesus to partake in the Lord's Supper and the invitation to each person in your family to learn more about the Lord's Supper in the days ahead. The remaining four days will help your family answer this question: What is the Lord's Supper all about?

Together, you will discover that it is

- a way to see, smell, taste, touch, and hear God's love.

- a very special gift.

- a way to remember.

- a reminder that we belong.

God's gift of the Lord's Supper is both incredibly simple and incredibly complex. To help children (and adults!) make connections between what they already know and what they are learning, we've used familiar objects in each devotion—an invitation, packages of food, a family photo, presents, and even the idea behind a "sacrifice fly" in a baseball game.

We also included "Faith Talk" ideas to help your family enter into a time of conversation and wondering together. And, for those adults who like to dig a little deeper, we've provided "A Closer Look" reflections on each of the devotions, along with some questions and answers from the Heidelberg Catechism.

During some of the devotions your child is invited to add details to an illustration or draw one of his or her own. If you have more than one child or would like to use this book over and over again, you can use your own paper and staple or paper clip the drawings into the book. By saving your child's artwork in that way, each time you use this book you'll be able to see how your family's understanding of the Lord's Supper has deepened over the years!

It's our prayer that as you read through these devotions together you will understand—while standing back in awe—a little more about God's great invitation to "Come to the table!"

You're Invited!

Jesus invites you to come to the table
and share in his special meal for his family.

"Taste and see that the Lord is good;
blessed is the one who takes refuge in him."

Psalm 34:8

An Invitation from Jesus

BEFORE YOU BEGIN

- Bookmark your Bible to Psalm 34, or invite a child to locate the passage and bookmark it for you.

READ TOGETHER

"Come to the table!"

Hot dogs and french fries . . . veggies and dip . . . deep-dish pizza melting with mozzarella cheese—it doesn't matter what's on the menu when we're hungry. "Come to the table!" are the words we want to hear!

What's really amazing is that Jesus invites us to come to the table too— the Lord's Supper table—for a very special kind of meal. That special meal has many different names: the Lord's Supper, communion, the Eucharist, and the Mass. And each church serves this meal in different ways.

Have you ever wondered just what this meal is all about? Why the pastor holds up the food and drink and says special words? Why people eat pieces of bread and drink juice pressed from grapes? What people are thinking about as they eat the bread and drink the juice? And who is invited to join in Jesus' special meal?

We're going to talk about some of those questions together over the next few days. For now, we'll just answer the last one: Who is invited to join in Jesus' special meal? Everyone in God's family!

Think about the special family meals you may have been invited to—a birthday party, a wedding dinner, a meal after a baptism, an anniversary party, and more. Family celebrations are a wonderful time to get together and remember an important event. The Lord's Supper is a time when God's family gets together to celebrate and remember what God has done for us.

The very first Lord's Supper was held a long, long time ago. The night before he died, Jesus invited his followers, the disciples, to join him for a special meal. He wanted to give his followers a way to always remember just how much he loved them.

Jesus wants us to know and remember how much he loves us too! That's why Jesus invites all of his followers—everyone who believes in Jesus and is sorry for his or her sins—to celebrate the Lord's Supper in the same way today.

TRY THIS!

Look in a story Bible or online for an illustration of the first Lord's Supper. (Or search for *The Last Supper* by Leonardo da Vinci.) Talk about the details you see. What does it look like Jesus and the disciples are feeling? Which person might be Judas? Why? (See Mark 14:17-20 for that part of the story.) This story is often called "The Last Supper." Can you think of any other good titles?

For the next few days we're going to learn more together about the Lord's Supper and God's incredible love for us. But first, here's your invitation:

Read Psalm 34:8a.

FAITH TALK

(Use some or all of the following conversation starters.)

- Tell each other about a memory you have of a family meal or celebration.

- Why do you think Jesus chose a meal as a way for his followers to remember him?

- What words can you think of to describe the Lord's Supper?

- Is there anything else that you wonder about the Lord's Supper or Jesus' invitation?

PRAYER

Invite those who are present to respond after each line with, "Thank you, Jesus!"

> Dear Jesus, you love us so much.
> **Thank you, Jesus!**
> You came to earth for us.
> **Thank you, Jesus!**
> You died for us.
> **Thank you, Jesus!**
> You came back to life for us.
> **Thank you, Jesus!**
> And you gave us a wonderful way to remember how much you love us.
> **Thank you, Jesus!**
> Amen.

A Way to See, Smell, Taste, Touch, and Hear God's Love

BEFORE YOU BEGIN

- Gather a small amount of food for each person. (Use food from your kitchen cupboards, like crackers, bread, cereal, chocolate chips, mints, and so on. Or purchase a different candy treat for each person, such as M&M's, Skittles, Tic-Tacs, chips, etc.)

- Put each type of food in a brown paper lunch bag or another opaque container.

- Gather some pencils, pens, markers, or crayons for anyone who would like to draw the picture at the end of this devotional.

- Bookmark your Bible to Matthew 26:26-28, or invite a child to locate the passage and bookmark it for you.

One at a time, have each person close his or her eyes before you hand each a package of food (see above). Each person must guess what's inside his or her package by using his or her senses of touch, hearing, smell, taste, and, finally, sight.

READ TOGETHER

Our senses—seeing, smelling, touching, tasting, and hearing—are all ways God has given us to learn and understand so much about the world. Just think about how using your senses helped you guess (or come close to guessing) what was inside your mystery package!

Our senses help us understand another kind of mysterious food package—the plate of bread and the cup of juice that we see on the communion table in church. Sometimes we call this Lord's Supper package "the elements." Here's how the bread and juice were presented at the very first Lord's Supper:

> *Read Matthew 26:26-28.*

When we hear the pastor read Jesus' words and when we see, smell, touch, and taste the bread and juice, we remember and know how much God loves us.

God uses words to tell us how much he loves us. In the Bible, God says again and again,

> "I love you."
> "I loved you before you were born."
> "I love you as you grow up, and I give you all the good
> gifts of my creation."
> "I even love you when you make mistakes. Then my love
> is forgiveness."

But God also showed us how much he loves us by sending his Son, Jesus, to earth in a human body as a sweet, squirmy baby with a delightfully toothless smile. The Bible says in John 3:16, "For God so loved the world that he gave his one and only Son. . . ." Jesus is God's forgiving love made real . . . in the flesh.

God wants us to know with more than just our brains and our hearts that God's forgiveness is real and true. So God gave us the Lord's Supper as a way to see, smell, taste, touch, and hear God's forgiveness—to know with our whole bodies that we are loved by God through his Son, Jesus Christ.

FAITH TALK

(Use some or all of the following conversation starters.)

- How do you know God loves you?

- Tell about a favorite memory you have—a place you've been, something special you did with a friend or family member, or another event you enjoyed. What do you remember about what you saw, smelled, tasted, touched, or heard?

- God gave us the Lord's Supper so we could remember how much God loves us by seeing, smelling, tasting, touching, and hearing. Why is that so important?

- Do you remember the words Jesus said about the bread and the cup? (You might wish to reread them from Matthew 26:26-28.) What do you think they mean? What do you wonder about the bread and the cup used by your church?

- Is there anything else that you wonder about the Lord's Supper?

PRAYER

Echo these words:

> Dear Lord,
> Thank you for using food
> to help us remember
> how much you love us.
> We love you too.
> Amen.

Does your supper table look the same as the supper table at the home of your friends or other family members? The way each church sets the Lord's Supper table may look a little different too.

Draw a picture of what the bread and juice look like at your church. (If more than one person would like to draw a picture, add lines to divide up the drawing space.)

DAY 3

A Very Special Gift

BEFORE YOU BEGIN

- Get a pen or pencil.

- Bookmark your Bible to Ephesians 2:4-10, or ask a child to find and mark the passage.

Tell each other about the best present you ever opened.

READ TOGETHER

Most people like to get presents. It's exciting to get a gift wrapped in shiny paper, tied with a ribbon or topped with a bow, and to wonder about what might be inside. Do you think God likes presents? Of course God does! But what God likes best is giving them!

God filled the world with gifts for people to enjoy—amazing animals, tall trees, cool water, interesting sounds, incredible colors, and many other wonderful things. God gives each person special gifts too. Singing, drawing, playing sports, listening, sharing, and helping are just a few of the things that God might have given you the ability to do well. And, because God loves people so much, he sent his own Son, Jesus, to the world as the very greatest gift of all.

Have you ever heard someone say "Like father, like son" or "Like mother, like daughter" when a person does something that's just like his or her parent? Well, Jesus is just like his Father—he loves to give people great gifts too. Jesus gave his disciples the gift of a special supper as a way of showing that he loved them. The Lord's Supper is a gift for us to remember how much Jesus loves us too!

But there's even more to this gift! First, it's a gift of grace. Remember the present you talked about earlier? Imagine getting an even more incredible present when it's not your birthday or graduation or another special day—but just because someone loves you. Being forgiven by Jesus is an amazing gift because we didn't do anything to deserve it. That's what grace is like.

Second, through this Supper, Jesus gives himself to us by the power of his Holy Spirit. And it is the work of the Holy Spirit to "open" this gift for us, so that in our hearts we'll know that we are completely forgiven from all our sins.

> *Read Ephesians 2:4-10.*

When we eat the bread and drink from the cup at the Lord's Supper, we're remembering Jesus' incredible gift of grace. And we're showing our gratitude to God with our thank-you gifts of praise, songs, and prayers.

Gift, grace, and gratitude. Let's say those words together: gift, grace, gratitude. That's what communion is all about.

FAITH TALK

(Use some or all of the following conversation starters.)

- What are your favorite creation gifts from God? (List them in the spaces on this page.)

- Think about the special gifts and abilities that God has given to the people in your family. Name one special ability God gave to the person sitting beside you. (List these too!)

- What does it mean when someone says, "I forgive you"?

- We didn't do anything to deserve God's gift of Jesus, but God gave his Son anyway! What do you think about that?

- Is there anything we talked about today that you wonder about?

TIP

Two great children's picture books on the theme of grace are *All You Ever Need* by Max Lucado and *Sidney and Norman* by Phil Vischer.

GIFTS GOD GAVE US

_____

_____

_____

_____

_____

_____

_____

_____

_____

_____

_____

_____

PRAYER

Close with a "popcorn prayer." Explain that you will begin the prayer, then you'll pause in the middle so that anyone can jump in to name a gift from God for which he or she is thankful. Encourage everyone to join in more than once.

> Loving God,
> You gave us a world full of gifts to enjoy—animals,
> things to eat, places to go, and more!
> We'd like to thank you for some of those gifts now.
> Thank you for *[name something for which you are thankful and then pause for popcorn prayers to begin]*.
> And thank you most of all for the gift of grace you gave
> us by sending your Son, Jesus,
> to be born on earth,
> to die on a cross,
> to come back to life,
> and to return to heaven to live with you.
> We love you, Lord!
> Amen.

DAY 4

A Way to Remember

BEFORE YOU BEGIN

- Find a family photo or several other photos featuring the people who are present for this devotional. (Even a photo on your cell phone will do!)

- Get a pen or pencil.

- Bookmark your Bible to 1 Corinthians 11:23-26, or ask a child to find and mark the passage.

- Optional: find a praise-song video online if you'd like to watch one together as your closing prayer.

> Look at the photo(s) together. Invite each person to tell what he or she remembers about when the picture was taken. (If there is someone who is too young to recall any details, share your own memory of that person on that day.)

READ TOGETHER

Pictures help us remember the things people in our family have done. The Lord's Supper is a way for the people in God's family to remember what Jesus has done.

Many years before Jesus died on the cross, God's people, the Israelites, were slaves in Egypt. The night before they escaped, God told them to sacrifice a perfect lamb and spread its blood on the doorframes of their homes so that they would be protected from the plague of death God was sending to the Egyptians. After that, the Israelites kept sacrificing perfect lambs as a way of remembering that God had saved them. They did this for many years, right up until Jesus came.

Jesus is called the "Lamb of God" because he sacrificed his life to take away the sin of the world and save us from the worst kind of slavery—the slavery to sin and death. When we eat the bread and drink the juice from the cup, we remember that we are set free from sin to be the children of God.

Like the Israelites, we all sin every day. We hurt other people and ourselves and God's creation. Does that make you feel sad? That's OK! We should feel sad about our sin and the ways we disobey God.

But we also have a reason to feel very glad. God has given us a way for our sins to be completely forgiven! God sent Jesus to be the final sacrifice. Like the lambs the Israelites used to sacrifice day after day, Jesus is the one and only perfect Lamb that could—and did—and does—take away our sin forever!

At the very first Lord's Supper, Jesus told his disciples how to remember him. Here's how an early church leader named Paul describes what happened:

Read 1 Corinthians 11:23-26.

During the Lord's Supper at church, the pastor holds up the communion bread and the juice as a reminder to everyone that Jesus gave his own body and shed his own blood on the cross as a sacrifice for us. And when it's time to eat the bread and drink the juice, the pastor might use words like these to help us remember Jesus' sacrifice for us: "The body of Christ, given for you" and "The blood of Christ, shed for you."

Jesus died so our sins could be forgiven, and Jesus rose from the dead to *prove* they are forgiven. That's something too important to ever forget!

TIP

To help your child understand the concept of sacrifice, you can explain that it means to give up something important for a good reason or for the sake of someone else. (If your child is familiar with baseball, you might talk about the reason behind a "sacrifice fly" as a way to help him or her make a connection.) There's also a helpful children's book on the topic of sacrifice—check your local library for *The Giving Tree* by Shel Silverstein.

FAITH TALK

(Use some or all of the following conversation starters.)

- Tell about a memory you have of a Lord's Supper celebration at your church or another church you were visiting.

- What would you say if someone asked what communion helps you remember?

- When you make a sacrifice for someone, it means you are giving up something for that person. Tell about a time you made a sacrifice for someone or a time when someone made a sacrifice for you. How did that feel?

- Have you ever had someone tell you to "prove it" when you said you had done or could do something? When Jesus came back to life after dying on the cross, he proved that he was God's Son and that he was able to forgive our sins. How does having that proof make you feel? Why?

- Is there anything we talked about today that you wonder about?

PRAYER

Sing a favorite song of praise (or several songs!) as your closing prayer for today, or watch a praise-song video together online.

Many churches have a special table on which to place the bread and juice for the Lord's Supper. Sometimes the special table has words carved into the front. Does your church have a table like that? If so, what does it say on the table? If not, what words about remembering would you carve in the table if you could? Add those words to the table on this page.

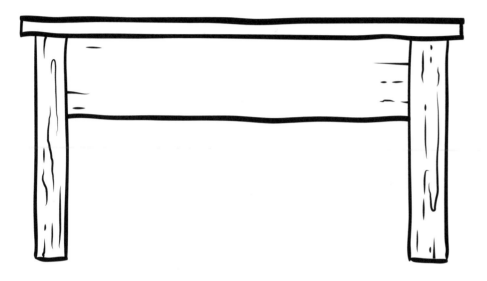

A Reminder That We Belong

BEFORE YOU BEGIN

- Bookmark your Bible to 1 Corinthians 10:16-17, or ask a child to find and mark the passage.

It's time for a quick quiz! Name one answer for each question, or shout out as many answers as you can—it's up to you!

Name a town or city. The people who live in [*place or places you named*] are part of a community because they live in the same area.

Name a school. The children and teachers who go to [*school or schools you named*] are part of a community because they belong to the same school.

Name a sports team. The players on [*team or teams you named*] are part of a community because they play together on a team. Their fans are part of a community too—a community of people who cheer for the same team!

READ TOGETHER

A *community* is a group of people who live in the same area or who have something in common with each other. Can you name some of the communities to which you belong?

Did you name your church? It's a community of believers—people who believe that God sent his Son, Jesus, to earth to die for our sins and make us into new people who love God and who love each other. The amazing thing about this community of believers is that it's spread across the entire world! And this community has a special name: *the body of Christ.*

Your body has many different parts—arms, legs, eyes, ears, teeth, knees, elbows, and more. These parts work together so you can do all kinds of things. The church is filled with different people of all sizes, ages, and abilities. Together, all these different people function like one body. Each person—including you!—is a part of that body. Isn't that wonderful?

Read 1 Corinthians 10:16-17.

The bread that we share during the Lord's Supper reminds us that we are all part of the same body. And when we eat the bread and drink the juice, Jesus, through his Holy Spirit, becomes part of us and strengthens us— kind of like the way the food we eat becomes part of us and strengthens us. Exactly how that happens is a mystery to us—but not to Jesus!

Next time you're in church, look around. Whom do you see? Is your friend grinning at you from across the aisle? Is your favorite Sunday school teacher a few seats back? Can you see the older couple who often sit ahead of you? Do you see the baby who was baptized a few weeks ago? How about the person who shook your hand last Sunday? Do you see people you love and who love you too? You're all an important part of your church community and the body of Christ. Celebrating the Lord's Supper is a way Jesus tells us that we belong to him, that he lives in us, and that we also belong to each other as members of the body of Christ.

The next time your church community celebrates the Lord's Supper, think about this amazing fact: at the same time that your church is celebrating the Lord's Supper, hundreds of thousands of other communities of believers are doing the same thing!

Imagine how Jesus feels about that!

TRY THIS!

Search the Internet to see how big the community of believers is around the world. (A word or image search of "Christians around the world" should yield good results.) Pray for places where there are few believers. And pray that God will help your family to share Jesus' love in the communities to which you belong.

28

FAITH TALK

(Use some or all of the following conversation starters.)

- Tell about a time when someone in your church community helped you or showed love to you.

- How is your church community like a family? How is the Lord's Supper like a family meal?

- Stand beside each other and practice the following movements together until you can do them at exactly the same time: *step to the right, put your hands on your hips, bend over, stand up, and clap three times.* When you're finished, give God a "Yay, God!" shout of praise for creating you to work together as one body.

- You are part of God's family in your church and you are part of God's enormous family around the world and in heaven. How does that make you feel? Why?

- Today we talked about how we belong to a community of believers. There is another word for the Lord's Supper that sounds like community. What is it? Why do you think the Lord's Supper might also be called *communion*?

- Is there anything else we talked about today that you wonder about?

PRAYER

Join with the worldwide community of believers today as you pray the Lord's Prayer together. (If it's not familiar to everyone, say it as an echo prayer so that each person can join in.)

Our Father in heaven,
hallowed be your name.
Your kingdom come.
your will be done,
on earth as it is in heaven.
Give us this day our daily bread.
and forgive us our debts,
as we also have forgiven our debtors.
And lead us not into temptation,
but deliver us from the evil one.
For yours is the kingdom
and the power
and the glory forever. Amen.

People come in all shapes and sizes—and so do church buildings!

What does your church building look like? Draw it here by having each person in your family draw one part of the building—doors, windows, the sign, and so on. When you're finished, all your different parts should make up one whole church!

A Closer Look . . .

Adults, if you want to dig deeper into
exploring the Lord's Supper, use the
following reflections in addition to the
preceding readings.

A Closer Look . . .

AN INVITATION FROM JESUS

This devotional is about a very special meal, a feast actually. You might even call it a party. And we begin where every special occasion begins, with an invitation.

Just before the Lord's Supper in many Reformed churches, after all the preparatory teaching and prayers of blessing and thanksgiving, the pastor says something like this: "The gifts of God for the people of God. Come with gladness to the table of the Lord." In this feast Jesus Christ himself invites his baptized people to come to this festival of grace, this table of forgiveness, this kingdom party.

Who exactly is invited? The church has always been careful not to make this invitation completely open. First of all, it's for baptized people. In our baptism we have been united with Christ in his death and resurrection. This is a meal to encourage, strengthen, and nourish the baptized.

But it's not just for the baptized; it's also for baptized believers. In other words, to come to the table, we need faith that Jesus loves us, died for us, and wants to live in us. The invitation is for those who, however haltingly, however imperfectly, trust in Jesus for their salvation.

This devotional is meant to help you invite your child (or children) to the table and/or to prepare your family for a communion celebration at any time during the year. In recent decades, most Reformed churches have taken the position that our baptized children belong at the table along with the whole community. Just as children participated in the feasts of ancient Israel, such as the Passover, our children belong at the Lord's Supper. They are baptized and they have faith—a childlike but very real faith. Through the experience of participation from an early age, their faith will grow and their understanding of the meaning of the sacrament will deepen.

What a blessing it is for our children to join the whole congregation at the table of the Lord. What an encouragement this is for their faith. How wonderful for them to have that "hands-on" reality of the sacramental meal to nourish their tender but very real faith in Jesus.

And what a blessing it is for you to help them hear that invitation from the Lord—and in helping them hear it, to hear it again yourself with renewed faith and understanding.

A Closer Look . . .

A WAY TO SEE, SMELL, TASTE, TOUCH, AND HEAR GOD'S LOVE

Throughout "A Closer Look" you will read some important, and perhaps surprising, insights about the sacrament from the Heidelberg Catechism and the Belgic Confession. These confessions serve as a guide and standard for faith and doctrine in many Reformed churches. How to understand the sacraments, and particularly, the Lord's Supper, was a hot issue back in the sixteenth century when these confessions were written.

It's striking, then, that many Reformed Christians are surprised when they find out what the old confessions really say. They teach us that the sacraments are far more important in our faith formation than we typically think. They especially emphasize how God makes himself known to us in the sacraments in such human (even childlike) and multisensory ways.

Q&A 75

**How does the holy supper
remind and assure you
that you share in
Christ's one sacrifice on the cross
and in all his benefits?**

In this way:

> Christ has commanded me and all believers
> to eat this broken bread and to drink this cup
> in remembrance of him.
> With this command come these promises:

First,

> as surely as I see with my eyes
>   the bread of the Lord broken for me
>   and the cup shared with me,
> so surely
>   his body was offered and broken for me
>   and his blood poured out for me
>   on the cross.

Second,

> as surely as
>   I receive from the hand of the one who serves,
>   and taste with my mouth
>   the bread and cup of the Lord,
>   given me as sure signs of Christ's body and blood,
> so surely
>   he nourishes and refreshes my soul for eternal life
>   with his crucified body and poured-out blood.

Some Christian denominations see the bread and the cup as merely signs or symbols that remind us of Christ's sacrifice for our sins. Others teach that the bread and wine actually become the body and blood of the Lord.

Reformed teaching on the Supper stands somewhere in-between. Here's how Q&A 78 from the Heidelberg Catechism describes it.

Q&A 78

Do the bread and wine become the real body and blood of Christ?

No.

> Just as the water of baptism
>   is not changed into Christ's blood

and does not itself wash away sins
    but is simply a divine sign and assurance of these things,
so too the holy bread of the Lord's Supper
    does not become the actual body of Christ
    even though it is called the body of Christ
        in keeping with the nature and language of sacraments.

On the one hand, the bread and wine do not somehow become the actual or physical body and blood of Christ. On the other hand, they are not merely signs or symbols for us to remember what Christ did for us.

The Reformed position is that the bread and wine of the sacrament of the Supper are not only signs or symbols, but also *seals* that make God's promise of grace tangible for us. They not only remind us but also assure us of God's grace in Christ.

Q&A 66

What are sacraments?

Sacraments are visible, holy signs and seals.
They were instituted by God so that
    by our use of them
he might make us understand more clearly
    the promise of the gospel,
and seal that promise.

And this is God's gospel promise:
    to grant us forgiveness of sins and eternal life
        by grace
        because of Christ's one sacrifice
        accomplished on the cross.

We also believe that Jesus is spiritually present in the Supper. This means that as surely as we see, touch, and taste the bread and wine in faith, so surely are we receiving Christ himself and all his blessings. Here's how the Belgic Confession states it: "Yet we do not go wrong when we say that what is eaten is Christ's own natural body and what is drunk is his own blood—but the manner in which we eat it is not by the mouth, but by the Spirit through faith" (Article 36).

A Closer Look . . .

A VERY SPECIAL GIFT

The word *sacrament* comes from a Latin term that means *mystery*. That's appropriate in the sense that no one really understands the sacraments and how they operate. They are mysteries. The Belgic Confession tells us that though we certainly trust that Christ comes to us in the sacrament of communion, "the manner in which he does it goes beyond our understanding and is incomprehensible to us, just as the operation of God's Spirit is hidden and incomprehensible" (Article 36).

Still, we wonder, how do these earthly elements unite us with Christ? The special blessing of the Lord's Supper is that we are invited to believe in Christ through the visible, tangible elements of bread and wine. These physical elements are meant to strengthen our faith, to give it a solid grounding.

Reread Q&A 75 (see "A Closer Look," Day 2). If you trust in Jesus as your Lord and Savior, no matter how weak your faith may be, the Spirit of God assures you that Christ is present in the Supper and in your life always.

So at the table you can open your heart to receive this gift: to know that you are forgiven and that Christ who is alive in heaven is also alive in your heart.

A Closer Look . . .

A WAY TO REMEMBER

In many congregations the Lord's Supper tends to be a rather somber occasion. And, in a sense, it ought to be. As the apostle Paul reminds us, in the Supper we "proclaim the Lord's death until he comes" (1 Cor. 11:26).

The Supper includes a remembering of the death of the only true and perfect human being who ever lived—and who died because of our sins. This public remembering or proclaiming of his death for our sin, Jesus said, must never end until he comes again.

But the Lord's Supper is also a joyous celebration of the resurrected and present Lord, who wholly covers our sins and draws us together as one community. The one who died is now risen, and the Holy Spirit unites us with our risen Lord, who now reigns in heaven. The Heidelberg Catechism captures both this penitence and joyful union with Christ.

Q&A 76

**What does it mean
to eat the crucified body of Christ
and to drink his poured-out blood?**

It means
  to accept with a believing heart
    the entire suffering and death of Christ

and thereby
   to receive forgiveness of sins and eternal life.

But it means more.
   Through the Holy Spirit, who lives both in Christ and in us,
   we are united more and more to Christ's blessed body.
      And so, although he is in heaven and we are on earth,
      we are flesh of his flesh and bone of his bone.
      And we forever live on and are governed by one Spirit,
         as the members of our body are by one soul.

This continuous remembering of both our sin and Christ's sacrificial
death cannot eliminate the celebration at the center of this feast. The
Lord's Supper keeps us from falling into two ditches: self-righteousness
on the one hand or insecurity on the other.

In other words, we are reminded at each Supper that our invitation to
come with confidence to the table of the Lord is based exclusively on
the sacrificial love of Christ.

Q&A 81

Who should come to the Lord's table?

Those who are displeased with themselves
   because of their sins,
but who nevertheless trust
   that their sins are pardoned
   and that their remaining weakness is covered
      by the suffering and death of Christ,
and who also desire more and more
   to strengthen their faith
   and to lead a better life.

Hypocrites and those who are unrepentant, however,
eat and drink judgment on themselves.

A Closer Look . . .

A REMINDER THAT WE BELONG

Each year during Holy Week (the seven days from Palm Sunday through Easter) we especially commemorate the time Jesus first celebrated the Supper with his disciples. We call that day *Maundy Thursday.* The term *Maundy* comes from the Latin word *mandatum,* from which we get the English word *mandate,* or *command.* This term comes from Jesus' own words on that very night.

After demonstrating the "full extent" of his sacrificial love to his disciples by washing their feet, Jesus tells them: "A new command I give you: Love one another. As I have loved you, so you must love one another. By this everyone will know that you are my disciples, if you love one another" (John 13:34-35).

That means that the first Supper—and every Supper since—displayed not only the Father's infinite love for humanity in the sacrifice of his Son, but also God's command and expectation that this same love would continue to circulate in the community of believers.

Read Q&A 76 again (see "A Closer Look," Day 4). The Lord's Supper is much more than a personal means of grace meant for each of us individually. It is a reminder of and a call to be a community of love. As Paul says, "Because there is one loaf, we, who are many, are one body, for we all share the one loaf" (1 Cor. 10:17). In the very next chapter, Paul reprimands the church for its callousness to the poor. He says that the Corinthians are not "discerning the body" of Christ (11:17-34).

How can we be unforgiving or hold grudges or turn our backs on those with whom we share in the body and blood of Christ? When Christ offers us his body and blood in the sacrament of communion, he also makes us into one body in him. In the Lord's Supper this becomes vividly real.